EVERYTHING
IS REAL

EVERYTHING IS REAL

POEMS

BY

RITA FEINSTEIN

Brain Mill Press
Green Bay, Wisconsin

Many thanks to the following publications for giving these poems their first homes:

The Cossack Review: "Lunch with Lancelot"
Hypertrophic Literary: "Skin" (published as "My Imaginary Lover Lives in a White House")
The Barrelhouse Blog: "The Imaginary Lover Toxicity Scale," "To Break the Curse"
Queen Mob's Teahouse: "Dream Journal"
Permafrost Magazine: "Revelation Comes as a Lightning Bolt," "Bow and Arrow"
Spry Literary Journal: "The Black Bull's Bride"
Cicada: "Medusa"
Okay Donkey: "The Goblin King's Love Language"
Blue Earth Review: "Instructions for Sex Dream Intern," "Balsamic Moon" (published as "It's Always the Moon")
miniskirt magazine: "My Monster Slayer"
trampset: "The Sphinx's Bride"
The Normal School: "My Imaginary Lover Breeds Dragons" (full sequence)

Published in the United States by Brain Mill Press.
Print ISBN 978-1-948559-76-8
EPUB ISBN 978-1-948559-77-5
MOBI ISBN 978-1-948559-78-2
PDF ISBN 978-1-948559-80-5

Cover design by Ampersand Book Covers.

www.brainmillpress.com

To all my loves, both real and imaginary.

"Everything you can imagine is real."

—PABLO PICASSO

Contents

Creation Myth

It started with shadowboxes,
tissue paper skies and tinfoil stars,
sloppy edges glopped in glue.

But soon I learned to approximate
northern lights reflected in ice,
honeysuckle climbing cracked stucco,

the shadow of a dragon's wings
passing over a prairie floodplain.

I shelved my craft scissors and began
kneading the molecules with my bare hands.

The boxes outgrew their cardboard frames,
developed their own weather patterns,
biomes, centers of gravity.

Nights here were starrier but colder
so I imagined a lover to warm the bed.

I pulled him from the water like Excalibur.
His uncut hair wrote dark scripture down his back.

Naked, he knelt before the castle
I'd built from lust and river rock.
He laid his shield in the reeds.

The world created man
who created god
who created man.

All creation starts with love.
And/or violence.

Skin

i.

His name is Daniel. Alexander. Nicolas. Laurence.
He's the pirate king and he skins selkies for sport.
I can hear them on the beach at night—
all those women crying to become seals again.

ii.

He cooks for me,
carpaccio with crostini
and horseradish foam.
He slices the fish so thin
I could break it with my breath.
It tastes like blood-wet velvet,
like just the smell of it
could drown me.

iii.

He calls me lioness.
He calls me honey,
my name throbbing
in his throat.
He lays me on his white bed
and in his hands
I'm an ecstasy of seafoam
sparkling as I shatter.

iv.

If I could I'd be a selkie
just to feel his hands inside me,

to be a human heart
beating inside sealskin.
I want him to cut me open.
I want him to whisper not to fight.

The Imaginary Lover*
Even Better Than the Real Thing!

Voted best romantic getaway since 2003, the imaginary lover offers a variety of erotic escapes, and all from the comfort of your own bed. User-friendly and fully customizable, the lover is suitable for all ages (18+) and experience levels.

Now in his 12th Anniversary Edition, the lover has been programmed with nine provocative new features, including "Crooked Grin" and "Troubled Past," as well as a variety of toe-curling adventure packages. Choose from perennial favorites like "Help! My Prom Date Is a Vampire!" and "Set Upon by Brigands, Then Ravished by the Roadside;" or, if you really want to steam up the windows, upgrade to Premium to try your hand at "Sacrificial Virgin."**

Safe for you and the environment, the imaginary lover is quality-controlled and never tested on animals. Experts agree that the imaginary lover is an effective, noninvasive technique for increasing libido, improving appetite, and stimulating creative cognition.

This holiday season, discover a world of pleasure and possibility with the imaginary lover. It's never felt so nice to be naughty!

---

*   Not recommended for long-term use (see "The Imaginary Lover Toxicity Scale").

**   Act now and receive a "Dragon Breeding Ranch" promotional package at no additional cost!

My Monster Slayer

is deep-keeled, swarthy as hell,
so fucking huge he keeps wearing
through his leather brigandines.

I always snickered at swolness—
poor gorillas can't touch their toes—
always fell for sapling boys,

but my slayer's old-growth girth,
lightning-split and lichen-fleeced,
fills my mouth with sap.

Each morning he deadlifts planets,
drinks a lake of protein shake,
showers in buffalo sweat,

but at night he cups me in his palms,
trembling with the effort of gentleness.
He'd fall to his knees if he crushed me,

and the world would fall with him.
So then tell me, lover, slayer,
which one of us is stronger?

My Imaginary Lover Says There's a Dinosaur

in a cave deep inside the mesa,
sleeping on her belly in the warm silt,
submerged up to her steaming nostrils.

She's been that way for centuries,
her heart beating once a minute,
her flanks swelling and sinking
as slow as the tides.

He says one drop of her blood
could fill a cup. Its iron has an undertow
of chocolate, like a salted mocha,
and a taste of it would drive you mad

with inspiration—you'd eureka yourself to death
painting angels in the sky.
He says he'd bring me her blood
if that's what I wanted, even if it killed me,

even if it killed him. He says he dreams
about standing next to that great golden eye
as it opens, pupil dilating
to swallow him whole.

My Imaginary Lover Is an Egyptian Mongoose

Smooth
as a swallow of water
he squirms

down my throat
while I sleep,
touching me

in ways I never
thought possible.

He plucks my heart
from its altar.

He will not
make it out alive
with this treasure

but it is not
escape he wants.

He eats the thing
whole, curls
in its gory hollow,

a weight that
in time
will feel familiar.

My Imaginary Lover Breeds Dragons (i)

He takes me to a horseshoe of riverbank, the sand scattershot with crayfish bits. We tiptoe through them to where eggs the size of papayas gather algae in the shallows. He says they'll have steel lungs and eyes like headlamps, and they'll cut through pressurized ocean trenches, fetching treasure from wrecks.

He says we'll finally fix up my old typewriter and put it by a window facing the ocean, and every night we'll have feta cheese and white wine and I'll never have to work in a donut shop again.

He says not to worry. He says we'll be a beautiful family.

He lifts an egg from the water and presses it, dripping, against my stomach.

The Peach

The night I create him,
my heart's pitted stone
swells with dimpled flesh,
then drops inside my hips
with a ripe thud.

I fumble for it in the dark,
but it's lodged deep.
It won't rot or soften
and it won't be harvested.

By midnight, it juices itself
to a bitter pip. A tiny fist
knocking against bone.

It beats beseechingly
till he plucks it free.

Every night I reimagine him.
Every night the peach grows again.

from My Imaginary Lover's Private Diary

after completion   you attack

     one another viciously

it pleases her

     this piercing

The Fox Bride

Once upon a time, all women were foxes and all men were hunters. The older the fox, the longer she had evaded capture, the more tails she grew. Our nine-tailed heroine made running look easy. No man had touched her, and precious few had seen her. She'd forsworn sleep years ago. She missed the dreams, but mostly she missed the nightmares. She'd forgotten the terror that first spurred her to run; now she couldn't stop if she wanted to. She was tired of running, and her beautiful tails were so heavy. She would have given them all for one night of torment. When she stepped into a bear trap, she thought she was finally dreaming. Once she might have chewed her own foot off, but she preferred the trap's sharp bite. She wondered how bad the pain could get. She wondered if she could keep pace with it. Patiently she waited as a bracelet of blood beads sprouted around her ankle. When the hunter entered the clearing, she welcomed him like her own demise.

Bow and Arrow

He takes me to a field at the end of my imagination,
where the dry thistles recede into emptiness
and the jaundiced sky threatens snow.
Seedheads cling to my leggings,
crackling like cicadas.

He hands me the recurve bow, molding my fingers
around the grip, fitting the arrow between
my knuckles. He stands behind me,
warm and supple as sapwood.

Without me he is empty; without him I am aimless.
But someday I will be both limb and missile.
I will be strong enough
to pull this string,

sharp enough to hit any target, even those I only
imagine are there. He presses my palm
to his heartbeat, so I will know
where to shoot, so that,
at the end

        I will make it fast.

Lunch with Lancelot

Everything is vegan but the way he looks at me.
I get the special, this beet-and-birdseed burger,
biodynamic farm-to-table buzzword buzzword.

He points at the tea menu and says *silver Ceylon*
with a smile that curls the server's hair.
He never seems to eat, but I've seen him

exquisitely torture a pear, carve it stem to calyx
and break the whole thing open like a flower.
I collapse in ripe slices when he says my name.

I'm supposed to be upset with him, with how
I died when he galloped past my window,
how I floated down the river in a funeral barge

filled with white lilies and washed ashore at his feet.
Why did you wait till then, I ask him,
to tell me I was pretty?

The burger arrives like a bleeding purple heart,
and the server makes a gussying show of pouring his tea.
He waits for her to leave, probably to die.

That's one version, he says. *In another
you were the queen, and we rode away from the flames
where your own husband condemned you to burn.*

He sips his tea, and his next words are sharpened
paring knives. *Don't you prefer it that way?*
I imagine my arms around his armored waist,

stale flames panting at our backs, an ending
anyone could want.
I shake my head *no*. I'm dizzy-hungry

and it feels like flying. I shake my head *no,*
because *How will I know you're real*
if you're not strong enough

to destroy me?
How indeed? he says, and I brace myself
for the knowing.

This Is What It's Like to Be Real

Not that grand, not that much
of a canyon either—

the abyss just something hollow
for the wind to moan through,

the rim a dry line
dividing empty from empty,

the sky a scraped-out socket
of hot, blind blue.

This Is What It's Like to Be Imagined

Now it's my turn, my imaginary lover says,
leading me through his butterfly pavilion.

Sunset streams through the honeycombed glass.
Red admirals rise from the catmint, wing tips

kissing my cheeks. He leads me to a blooming
fig tree, a chrysalis the size of a coffin

hanging open among its branches.
He throws me inside and shuts the door.

‡

I scream until my throat rattles
like a papery husk.

‡

Drenched in pale green blood, I step
from the broken shell, wet wings

plastered to my back. They dry
with a hard sheen, crackling

when he pins them to corkboard.
He runs his hands over the chitin

as if smoothing maps. Pleasure and pain
shimmer through membrane.

Stop, I cry, straining against the pins.
He tucks my hair behind my ear

and he whispers to me,
Don't you want to be this beautiful?

I Imagine Myself as the Kind of Girl My Imaginary Lover Would Love

I scrape off all the fat,
make a trellis of my ribs.

I fill myself with flowers,
honeysuckle and hollyhocks
with delicate throats
fit to swallow only sunlight.

Look at me in full bloom—
a skeleton slashed with open mouths.

My Imaginary Lover Breeds Dragons (ii)

He fetches his future brood queen from her atrium, ties her to his leather falconry glove with a length of chain. Her hatchling wingspan is wider than he is tall, her bone structure batty and underfleshed.

She flaps madly skyward, the sun slicking her black scales and blood-purple membranes. Her cries sound like peacocks being plucked alive.

"She's quite tame," he says, though his lean arms are iridescent with scars.

He grins like a boy with a kite, laughing when she nearly lifts him off the ground.

Slackening the line, he allows her to beat toward freedom, then abruptly grabs a cruel fistful of chain, nearly snapping her neck. Still she fights him, her screams turned to bruises in her throat.

"Someday," my lover says, "she'll realize there's nothing else out there."

He looks at me so suddenly that I return to my body in pins and needles. For a moment there, I'd forgotten I exist.

The Black Bull's Bride

Once upon a time a girl wished for true love, and who should come knocking at her door but a black bull? They were wed that night in a circle of Joshua trees. She insisted it was a mistake, cried off all her sugar skull makeup, tried to hurl her heart against the thorns. She carried on like this until all the guests had gone home, until she was no longer able to stand. Despite herself, she wrapped her arms around the bull's glistening neck. His throat pulsed like a vein of magma, and she knew it was her body that heated his blood. She shuddered and lay still against him, her fury blown from her body by the Sonora wind. Above her head, the wedding ring swung from his septum like a hollow moon, so big she'd have to wear it as a collar.

The Goblin King's Love Language

is gift-giving, and I don't have room for all this crap.
Psilocybic peaches rotting in the crisper,
crystal balls sticky with grime.

The black snake shriveled to onionskin,
the wedding dress sulking unworn
at the very back of the walk-in closet.

Goodwill stops taking my donations.
My free boxes overflow onto the sidewalk.
There's a landfill named after me,

a whole shuttle full of glitter-drenched
padded jackets and danger-red lipsticks
to be incinerated in the vacuum of space.

But I accept the love he gives, and I build
more shelving units for it, just as he accepts
my affection has no physical dimensions.

My love language is language itself.
I incant his name into my vanity mirror,
lie that he has no power over me,

then watch him jigsaw the stars
into brand-new horoscopes
just to prove me wrong.

Balsamic Moon

my imaginary lover is not a woman
but sometimes she appears to me

on a red slate rooftop   waves
of ivy splashing   up the walls

our footing precarious   our hands
almost   but never quite   touching

her nails little blue   moon phases
it's always the moon   isn't it

and when i ask her who
she fangirls   over hardest

she redbrick-blushes
and says   you

and what beautiful
miyazaki movie bullshit is this

a white cat   swirling like smoke
between the chimneystacks

i'm coming   of age
in summer   so magic

so clear   she and my lover
are the same   same sexy

librarian glasses   same shock
of black cherry hair   cut short for summer

same moon phase as when i was born
gibbous   balsamic   25° cancer

a late   as my astrologer said
bloomer

Instructions for Sex Dream Intern

PROFESSIONAL CONDUCT

Recommended attire is
    (1) vampy leather jackets with popped collars
        a. bloodstains on the cuffs
        b. and the corner of your mouth
    (2) contact lenses
        a. the shocking blue of rotten ice

Acceptable headwear includes
    (1)   harvest moon as a saint's aureole
    (2)   antlers sheathed in velvet

You may assume the likeness of
    (1)   my unrequited grad school crush
    (2)   a roguish misanthrope (Appendix C)
    (3)   Bono circa *The Joshua Tree*

But never (see also: fireable offenses)
    (1)   current or former students
    (2)   Bono circa *No Line on the Horizon*
    (3)   the roommate who drank all my wine

ADMINISTRATIVE DUTIES

Daily office tasks include
    (1) breathing lustily into phones
    (2) managing social media accounts (#sleepslut
        #snoregasm)
    (3) sending inappropriate photocopies

(4) backhanding everything off the desk, throwing me
    onto the warm cherrywood, ripping open my blouse

CONFIDENTIALITY CLAUSE

You may be asked to ride naked
on the furred seats of my vintage Volvo.

You may be asked to be an angel
made of painkillers and cloudbanks,
draping my chest with your wings.

NONDISCRIMINATION POLICY

Must be comfortable   with sexual organs
            changing kaleidoscopically
so that one of us   is always
            inside the other.

My Imaginary Lover Breeds Dragons (iii)

Dawn fills the valley like a punch bowl, all the evergreens chilled with dew. From our perch on an overhang, my lover and I watch the dragons' mating flight. The hatching sun makes their scales smolder like fire opals and milky jade. Pink chills rake my unarmored skin.

They're a knot of seething coils, throbbing like a heart. As they lash their tails together, something inside me starts to crack. A flaming mouth opens—my lover's tongue flicks against my neck.

He thrusts her deep into the sky. Their bodies quaking, pleasure sluicing through mine. My lover tearing my shirt like eggskin.

A silent roar shakes the dewdrops from the needles. All the tension hisses from my body. A wet yolk of light slides over the horizon.

Fenrir in Concert

His is the voice
that will eat the moon.
His mouth a shadow
falling over mine.
His chest
a wine cellar,
lungs unstoppered
in my ears.
All his words
in my mouth
but god I wish
his tongue was too.
God I wish he'd
eat me instead.
I follow him
like a satellite,
appetite
in perigee.
So close to earth
I make the waves
in his hair.
Hair like a splash
of amber beer.
Voice that could
fill a growler.
Voice like a comet
lacerating the atmosphere.
Voice of inevitable
impact.
Voice with
no encore.

My Imaginary Lover Enters My Bloodstream

Remember to breathe, he says.

---

i am waking up

and waking up

and waking up

like shedding   an orgasmic snakeskin

made of light

i am   omnidimensional

my mind honeycombing

far beyond   my body

i am waking up   and making sand angels

on the ocean floor   i remember to breathe   my breath

stokes me   like a salt fire

i fill   i flicker   i fracture into   satiny oblivion

my lover picks up   the pieces   my lover stitches every wound my lover is   beside me / inside me

          only our fingertips   touching

                    his blood pulses   in patterns like dragon scales

and i am as blue-green   as a nymph   i breathe   i wake

          i've never been

so far from my body   i've never

                                        loved it so much

Revelation Comes as a Lightning Bolt

I remember with perfect clarity the first time I met my lover's mother. Back then I was very sick, all my brown bones wrapped in paper. I felt so shabby beside her royal blue elegance.

Her desert casita was as wonder-stuffed as an old world bazaar, on every shelf a tangle of bangles or a beaky Turkish coffeepot. It was easy to imagine my lover growing up here, playing with runes instead of Legos.

Before lunch, she spread a piece of purple velvet on the table and shook a pack of tarot cards from its pouch. My lover vanished quietly into his room.

I drew The Tower—a lightning-seared spire in a blood-brown sky. On the ground below, crows tramped through carrion, meat hanging in rank whiskers from their beaks.

"What does this mean to you?" she asked.

"Disaster," I said, smiling to see something so familiar.

The Imaginary Lover Toxicity Scale

(1) Lover is harmless. Nameless and faceless, a composite rockstar with Adam Levine's forearms and young Bono's dark hair. In your indulgent loneliness, you stare at the light on your ceiling—its frosted globe and pewter nipple—thinking you feel that sturdy, that luminous, that electric when he's inside you, thinking you can hit the switch at any time.

(2) Lover always calls in his lunch order. You dread the phone but hope for his voice every time it rings. Sometimes you think he's flirting with you when he says, *kale salad, lightly dressed.*

(3) Lover's face was chiseled by angels. How could he love a moderately attractive girl like you? To get his attention, you put your fist through the boob light. You nearly drip to death before he binds your ragged flesh. *Sorry, clumsy,* you mutter, burning to punch it again.

(4) Lover has considerable virtuosity in the culinary arts. You wear a dress the jelly-jewel red of raw tuna, and he feeds you sashimi straight off the knife.

(5) Lover approves of your haircut, though he secretly wishes you'd gone blond. Over white wine and crab dip, you tell him he's imaginary. He looks at you like you're a canvas covered in paint balloons, like the only way he knows how to create is to destroy.

(6)   Lover gets into your bloodstream, and it feels like
        being hit in the head with a flower mallet. You wake
        up and daisies are rioting on the ceiling. You wake
        up and you're naked, spooning a dog. You wake up
        with super-vision; you can see beads of blood travel
        through his veins. You wake up with a devastating
        headache. You wake up cackling and speaking
        calmly at the same time, and you're not sure which
        voice is yours.

(7)   Lover hides a pea under your mattress. You are
        hysterical. You can't find it and you can't sleep.
        Friends and family won't say the pain you're feeling
        isn't real. Instead they will say, *I believe that you
        believe.*

Shark Dreams

Part of me believes it's a dolphin,
even as it seizes my outstretched hand
and starts to eat.

What does that say about you,
my lover asks, *that you just let it happen?*

Shaman wisdom says you must
fight the shark to become the shark.
Are you fighting? my lover asks.
Are you becoming?

Such questions are immaterial;
I have always been the shark.
I could betray him, destroy him
as easily as opening my eyes.

Recipes for the Apocalypse

While the sun blackens like a prune,
he makes me a tangerine quarantini
in a six-foot-diameter glass.
We drink it together, a straw on each side
of the apocalyptic orange rim.

While ash falls from a red moon,
he starts a porch garden,
sequins instead of soil,
five-gallon buckets brimming
with ripe crystal balls.

While lambs bleat in demonspeak,
we picnic at the cathedral garden
on grass so green it burns.
He eats a salad of obsidian chips
tossed in vinegar, and I unwrap
a crumbling supercontinent,
strawberry jam erupting
from the fault lines.

Isn't this what you wanted?
He shakes an empty pretzel bag,
and I dip my licked finger
in the salt crush and shards,
and yes—it does taste better
at the end.

Dream Journal

Last night, I dreamed I couldn't decide what to wear. Ultimately I picked out a dress, leggings, and an overshirt in different colors of plaid. The night before, I made an even worse mistake. I dreamed I brought you home with me and announced, in my best English accent, "We're going to bed!" My roommates were agog. Of all the people I could have imagined, they never imagined it would be you.

‡

If I told you I dreamed an evil kidney bean killed my favorite My Little Pony, you'd probably laugh. But now I know that danger can come from anywhere. Lover, I wonder how fast you can draw a gun.

‡

My dream dictionary has everything from *Abandoned Places* to *Zoos* but nothing that explains why I always feel like a maze of empty cages when I wake up. It tells me to "try to remember who or what aroused feelings of love or passion in [my] dream," but god, I'm trying to forget. That's why the cages are empty.

‡

They tell me it's unhealthy to spend so much time with you, so I make an imaginary friend too. She is ugly and obligatory and her name is Linda. I have always hated koalas and the color forest green, so I design her as such. We don't have anything in common. She's always eating melon balls and borrowing my clothes without asking. One day she spills eucalyptus oil on my plaid overshirt. "You bitch!" I cry, striking her across the face. She slaps me back, and we both laugh at the absurdity of the situation. Then you come home and shoot her between the eyes, killing her instantly. "I didn't like the way she was looking at you," you say. I weep inconsolably all night, face buried in my plaid shirt with its fading scent of eucalyptus.

‡

I used to tell myself, if only you murdered something I loved, I could stop loving you. Lover, it's not that simple. If anything, I love you more. It doesn't help that you learned to play "Even Better Than the Real Thing" on piano. I gasp as I'm plunged into the frosty notes of a song I no longer recognize and can't remember any other way.

‡

When I told my energy worker I loved Bono, she said the love we think we feel for other people is just misdirected love for ourselves. She also said her potted fern loves to be hugged.

‡

When I see a bat, I feel like it belongs inside my body. Like I'm not so much a zoo as a forgotten hibernaculum. Somewhere I heard that bats are drawn to ruined temples.

‡

You're in a coral button-up and dark-wash jeans, and I'm teaching you how to clear the bad energy from a room. You're a good listener, a real prodigy. *Spirits begone,* we say, clapping the shadows away. *Spirits begone.* But lover, do not clap at me. I am not done sleeping with you yet.

‡

Lover, I don't think you understand. Come inside me, and we'll talk.

Big Bad Wolf

When he welcomed me
into the house of his body,
I forgot what I'd been searching for.

In places I could see the bones,
rotten timbers peeking
through the plaster.

The wallpaper swelled gently
with his breath, and from the attic
came the beating of his dusty heart.

I could have let him sink
to his shattered foundation,
but I saw his potential.

I gutted the kitchen,
scrubbed till the linoleum
squeaked lemon-clean.

I'd found my purpose
in healing him. He was bad
so that I could be good.

I could have lived forever
inside him, but you
know the story.

The woodcutter and his axe,
the sudden blade biting
through flesh and drywall.

The callused hands
pulled me free, leaving
the best part of me inside him,

leaving a sack of wolfskin,
its stomach
a shredded red cape.

The Sphinx's Bride

Once upon a time there was a girl who was good at riddles. She solved her way across the world until she came to the mountain pass and beheld the terrible sphinx lording over his aerie of bones. His voice echoed like a fever dream, deafening, yet only in her head: *If a girl is in love with her own mind, which one of them is crazy?* The answer leapt into her mouth, but she bit it back, rolling it under her tongue like a morsel of raw lamb. Looking beyond his roost, she saw his fabled treasure—just a dead civilization, all its gods entombed in dust. She no longer wanted the reward. Not *that* reward. She sandaled closer to the great beast, gasping as his wings enfolded her like grape leaves. His eyes were the clear green of olive oil, a softness you could dip bread in. Did he take pleasure in his kills, she wondered, or was he fettered to a curse? Would the right answer doom him or cut him free? She touched his human face, his beautiful long hair. She whispered the answer in his ear.

To Break the Curse

Hold him as a millipede, shiny and striated
and wrapping itself up your arm. Hold him
as a glutinous pink squid with snapping beak
and flailing tentacles, as it spurts warm ink
on your face and clothes. Hold him as a hyena
foaming with fleas, a quenchless vampire bat,
a swarm of hornets. Hold him as nameless
atrocities, creatures you shouldn't be able to see
without a microscope. Hold him between
your knees as a bucking horse, as he grows
iron plating and leathery wings
and lungs that spew acrid yellow smoke.
Hold him as a dragon, as he shatters
a stand of sequoias with one sweep
of his studded tail. Between his scales, a dark,
smoldering mass like a bed of coals.
Hot to the touch—hold him as your palms blister
and the blisters burst. Hold him as he trips
over his own thrashing weight and into
the deep end of the lake. Hold him
as you're engulfed in steam, as his scales cool
and crumble like charcoal. Hold him till you feel
human fingers intertwine with your own.
Bob to the surface together in a cloud of debris.
Hold him knowing some sorceress somewhere
is very angry, that you've stolen what was hers.
Know this: the curse is broken but so are you.
He doesn't even know how much he hurt you.

Raise the Stakes

Me in a burgundy dress, him with an open wallet.
He orders me a cocktail called a quetzalcoatl
that burns a hole through my heart. He orders
everything on the menu, bottomless lotus blossoms
and winter lamb in pomegranate molasses.
He looks at me like he's spent twelve years in a bunker
and I am the world, still a green bowl of birdsong.
We could spend forever in this tender dénouement,
but every story must have conflict.

MAN VS. MAN

The waitress has an ass like a pomegranate
and I wouldn't be looking unless he was,
but now that I am, I feel like a broken plate,
which is not how I'm supposed to feel
when he's calling me *sweetheart* and squeezing
my thigh like a lime, but I worry sometimes
that I love him more than he loves me,
which means that either he has failed
or I have, and I envy the waitress
for the way she balances all those plates
on her arms, not even considering
the possibility of shattering.

MAN VS. NATURE

He's the last man on earth, if you
can call him that, and I am the last
woman, and everyone else

has been eaten by winged serpents
who erupt from the flagstone patio
like roots, but he thinks quickly
and grabs the knife from my lamb;
he slashes at their wrappings
but their skin is unripe and the knife
sleeks off in a rash of sparks,
and *I'm sorry*, he says,
it had to end like this.

MAN VS. HIMSELF

There is a hole in my heart
and it's filled with lime juice
and it's filled with snakes
and I don't know if I
would rather be the world
or eat it.

I don't know how this ends
but I know a story isn't real
until someone you love dies.

Field Journal Entry No. 1

Sometimes, when he thinks I'm not looking,
he points his fingers at me like a gun.

My Imaginary Lover Breeds Dragons (iv)

Jarnsaxa isn't like the other dragons. She looks me right in the eyes.

Named for a moon of Saturn named for a Norse giantess, she's all frost and fury, her white skin striped with vitriolic orange. When she sees me, she vomits sulfur at the gate of her enclosure. She butts her skull-face against the chicken wire, tongue wagging obscenely.

I have this idea that I can tame her, but I don't realize I've reached out until I hear a wet crack like a thunderclap. She would have ripped off my arm if my lover hadn't severed her head. The dripping jaws release, but I can feel their venom pulsing in the bite marks.

"Didn't you see the way she was looking at you?" my lover demands.

Yes, lover, of course I did. It's the same affectionate smile he gives me before tearing me apart.

He's agitated, his jaws worrying an imaginary bone. Without taking his eyes off me, he strokes the blood from his sword.

The Laws of Physics

(1)   I created him but he's destroying me.
(2)   He's not real but he cannot be destroyed.
(3)   Every imaginary lover has an equal and opposite
       imaginary girlfriend.

I name her Skye. Skye as in the atmosphere over Wyoming, where matter goes when it doesn't matter to anyone but me, a lawless frontier deviled with dust storms. Skye as in buzzards circling in her arid blue eyes.

She mirrors me in all ways but these: she likes the dry heat and the bloom of cream in her coffee. She sleeps in. Sleeps around. Sleeps with my imaginary lover. Bitch eats cantaloupe for breakfast.

I could kill her if she doesn't kill me first. I don't know who has the power here. She tells me if you're not part of the solution, you're part of the problem. I tell her you're the problem and you're part of me.

Is it voyeurism if I'm watching myself? Is it voyeurism if none of it is real, if the pleasure keeps shedding snakeskins of pain? She walks across the desert in dusty jeans, and he walks toward her with the sun at his back like a god. When they kiss my whole body starts peeling with desire.

How do I uncross this state line and return to the hotel room before she existed, the morning my imaginary lover woke me at dawn to hear the wolves? Now I'm alone in the room and the door won't lock, and the wolves are at the door, howling with her voice.

My Imaginary Lover Is a Vampire Who Must Be Destroyed

It could be simple as sushi dinner,
a chopstick plunged through his heart,

and yet I still let him roost in my body,
this woodrot coffin lined with red velvet.

I let him return to me each dawn,
glutted with blood that isn't mine.

My Imaginary Lover at Disneyland

FANTASYLAND

People keep asking what prince he is.
Mine, I think, clenching my fists

as he kneels before every little princess,
spinning stories about his marzipan castle,

his noble steed, and oh he's so good
with them that my womb wails

like a bright red klaxon,
stay out of my way, stay out

of me, but they will not run
and my lover has me

on a leash like a child—
a heartstring that burns

if I wander too far
from what he wants, which is

to make something permanent,
someone he can call his own,

but I never liked the sequels
about the heroine's daughter—

the brazen claim
that her parents' love story

is not, in fact, the only story
worth telling.

CLUB 33, NEW ORLEANS SQUARE

Bad decisions were made
over mint juleps

in a private lounge with lavender
wallpaper and lobster so rich

it flew here first class.
You knew what to whisper

into the hidden intercom,
and what to whisper in my ear

as your thumb rubs circles
on my inner thigh:

*If you love me, you'll let me
have this.* And oh, you devil,

you work your charms.
You plant the seed.

No sooner have I conceived it
than it is born.

TOONTOWN

She's a real fawn of a daughter,
the kind of beauty you can't
bring yourself to kill.

Who said anything about killing?
I only want to will her out of existence,
but my blood runs red and real in her veins—

my gift to her, stolen from me.
Her blood is real but her heart
is imaginary. Her heart belongs to him.

He follows her with his wallet,
buying up the whole park for her.
She eats while I starve

for him—gnawing the meat
from pink-brown turkey
or velociraptor drumsticks,

biting holes in everything
I worked so hard to build.
Tricksy pixie, I'm onto you.

Like me, you're a self-destruct button.
I know what you're thinking:
If I can't have him, no one can.

FRONTIERLAND

Lover, there's only one thing
more powerful than you,
and that's Child Protective Services,

circling down like buzzards,
squawking at you
to step away from the girl.

You were probably expecting me
to hand her a stick of dynamite,
but violence is not the only thing I do,

only the thing I do to you.
We're always cutting each other open,
you and I. We have the vivisection scars

to prove it. We're unfit parents
and she's not fit for this fantasy.
Lover, I did not spare her life

out of mercy. I did it to remind you
that I'm only as cruel as I need to be.
Lover, no one likes an evil queen.

MAIN STREET, U.S.A.

There's no amber alert
for a lost lover—

no one to help me find him
when he vanishes with a howl

and a surge of smoke.
The least he could do is burn

this whole world to the ground,
starting with me, for all witches

must burn, but the merry tinkle
of the afternoon finds him

reading the dedication plaque
at the gates of Tomorrowland,

a future so small it has only
five rides. To enter this land

is to enter uninhabitable grief.
To stay is to burn with me.

There is nowhere for him to go,
so my lover sinks slowly to his knees.

TOMORROWLAND

A vista into a world of [heedless deception],
signifying man's [failure] ... a [collapse]
into the future, with predictions of
[destruction] to come.

Tomorrow offers new frontiers in
[superstition, submission, and dissatisfaction]: [an] Atomic
[rage] ...
the challenge of outer space ... and the [fear of]
a [hostile] and [divided] world.

My Imaginary Lover Talks in His Sleep

please   it hurts

          get me out of

please just   go back

          go play   with your toys

                    your costumes

stop   wait   you can have everything

          you want   what do you want

everything   you wanted

          i have done   i am   exhausted

i can't live   within you

          what kind of girl   are you   you

should have given up   by now

He Pushes Me Through the Portal

A sob erupts from me
like a flushed pheasant
and before tripping
forward through time
the last thing I see
is redcoats falling
upon him like hounds
musketfire like bottles
breaking   but he
has escaped them
before and might do it
again   and it is
the not-knowing
that kills me   if only
it would kill me
and I hate him for this
which is   I think
what he intended
all along.

Jeopardy! Tournament of Champions

He knows how many scales on a juvenile pangolin
and what's on the other side of a black hole.

He knows med students practice abortion on papayas,
and pineapples practice vampirism on the human tongue.

His too-long finger rapid-fires the buzzer
before Trebek even reads the question.

Flames race up his wrist, around his shoulders,
a victor's mantle cinched with a smirking ember.

His competitors cower, their embarrassed
screens blushing with negative numbers,

as the live studio audience tweets from their seats,
asking questions no one has been able to answer,

and he calmly lays bare the universe's
most intimate secrets. His heterochromatic gaze

sees pastpresentfuture, sees everything but how
he and I will end, but bless his heart,

he knows that luna moths hatch without mouths,
mate, and starve to death in seven days.

The Stone Bride

Once upon a time there was a young wife whose husband never returned from sea. From a windswept precipice she watched his sails dissolve into evening. As the red drained from the sunset, so too did it drain from her heart, leaving only salt-stained rock. Grief stiffened her joints, and morning found her skin sheathed in a thin crust of chalcedony. There was still hope that he might come back, crack her open in a spill of quartz, but as night fell the crystals inside her went dark. She remained on the cliff, mistaking each wink of whitecaps for his homecoming sails. She waited so long the barnacles grew around her feet like boots. She waited until she couldn't have looked away if she wanted to. She was worshipped as a monument to faithfulness; young women crowned her with bleeding hearts, pledging fidelity, praying for patience. How could she tell them that she waited not out of love but out of vengeance? That she waited only to see his face when he saw what he'd done?

Postcard to My Imaginary Lover

Without you I'm a rabbithole,
a warren with no wonderland.

Bound

Dragonhide skinny jeans
with a belt of human teeth,
crow feather earrings, bloody smear
of lipstick on his wolfish grin.
I can't take him anywhere.

Descending from another night
of bondage mishaps, my body aches
like a leather couch studded with brass.
I could really go for a vanilla latte.

I stagger to the Starbucks
where my lover's brother works.
His all-black is clean and corporate,
his plumdark hair freshly cut
beneath the company-issue visor.
His smile doesn't hide any knives.
Immutably, he punches my loyalty card.

Later, I can't stop sexting him
pictures of the Eiffel Tower at dusk.
We meet at the rose garden,
the opera, the ice-skating rink.
It's been so long since I had a date
that didn't end with eating or being eaten.

I thought my lover would be livid,
but he just shrugs his bat wings
and fills his wine glass to the top.
He knows I'll come back to him eventually.
He's so bad to me, but when he's good,
I know he really means it.

My Imaginary Lover Saves My Life Again

Last week I nearly drowned, and just the other day I was buried alive. The first time I was clapped in a metal bikini and sex-slaved to a sentient gelatin, he didn't sleep until he found me. These days he takes his time, pulling over at cheap motels and windowless bars, watching distorted women through his whiskey glass, the way they debone their paper parasols and use what's left to pick the cherries from their teeth.

‡

He shatters my hourglass prison right before I'm smothered in sand. The shadowy fortress falls; the wicked sorcerer's bones scream to dust. With a weary kiss, my lover swings me onto his off-white steed. He's just glad it's over.

‡

I lay the traps, then I walk into them. I want to be saved, but I don't want to be safe. I make him hold me while I sweat out my fever dreams, then I take another dose of neurotoxin.

‡

It's too easy. That must be it. I adjust the settings, switch all the quests to evil mode. A labyrinth of bones, the floor paved with vipers, the ceiling with spiders. A seeping fog that whispers his own worthlessness to him. At the heart of the maze, identical copies of me poised in gallows and guillotines, strapped to racks and train tracks. If he saves the wrong one, he has to start all over.

My Imaginary Lover Is the Captain of a Spaceship

Light-years of hyperdrive
have changed the shape of his face.

His bone structure like the universe
is constantly expanding, too much

to hold onto. I can't compress him
into what he was before.

He's not looking for anything
so much as everything,

or his ability to experience it
all at once. He won't turn back

until he finds it. He'll keep sailing
long after the crew goes into cryosleep,

and I'll stand with him at the helm,
watching the nebulae bloom and die.

They say you stare into someone's eyes
long enough and you fall in love with them.

It's the same with deep space,
only after that you never look back.

My Imaginary Lover Breeds Dragons (v)

He names them after astronomical terms—Satellite and Betelgeuse, Azimuth and Ingress. They came from deep space, just like him. There's a cold weightlessness about them, the way they exist both in the world and above it. The way they look right through me.

"Here," says my lover, handing me a bowl of butchered chicken.

I take a wing, wrinkled with white fat, and wave it like a marshalling wand at Satellite. Even the sour savor of raw meat won't turn her head.

"I loved dragons before I even knew you," I pout.

"I'm not stopping you from loving them," he says.

Oh, but he is, and I know I can't have both. Dragons are too proud to settle for split hearts, and he has more than half of mine.

He can see I'm frustrated, so he takes the meat from me.

"Like this," he says, cupping a breast in his palm.

My Imaginary Lover Tells Me to Swallow

We have red cedar countertops,
bone-handled knives of carbon steel,
and eel steaks wrapped in wax paper,
so he makes sushi.

He broils the *unagi* golden-black,
swabs its underbelly with wasabi.

Its thick richness swells in my throat,
avocado, sriracha mayo, fatty fish.
My first taste of *too much*.

He splashes sesame oil in the pan,
feeds more eel to the heat.

Pain Manifesto

When you create a world, you create a mirror, all things microcosmic of their creator.

The problem with the world is that I created it.

In this world, there is no such thing as anger, only self-loathing and appropriate punishment.

The problem is that when I'm angry I want to destroy things, and the closest thing within reach is myself.

What is destruction but the creation of something broken?

One of these days I'd like to destroy something. Just to know what it feels like.

The problem is that all I know how to do is create.

The problem is that I'm made of glass—I have to be broken before I can cut.

Sometimes I wish my lover would break me to pieces.

Sometimes I want to hit him.

I believe he would hit harder if only I hit him first.

I believe that's why I created him.

Medusa

I wake up with the wind
slithering through my ribs.
Its tiny tongues tickle my heart,
the last lump of meat
in a skeleton picked clean.

I gave everything to him,
the prunes of my knuckles,
the purses of my lungs.

When all that's left
is snakes and bones,
you know it's time
to take yourself back.

I fill my veins with venom,
shepherd the serpents
to my skull.

Once their spines were vines,
their heads blossoms,
but now the only garden
is my plot of stone men,
calcified eyes open wide.

When my lover creeps in,
shield burnished like a mirror,
I will not look away.

I'm immune to my own poison.
I can't hurt myself anymore.

Tales of the Labyrinth

Once there was a queen who fell in love with a sacrificial bull. His eyes so trusting, his blood born to empty itself upon the altar. The cosmos itself was yoked to his shoulders, and without his planetary weight tilling the firmament, the cornflowers would stop blooming and the rains would cease to fall.

So the queen built a hollow wooden cow and locked herself inside until the bull came to mate. Months later she bore a son. Her heart swelled at the child's dear velvet face, the horns no bigger than pearls, the shoreline where fur met skin.

The king raged at her betrayal. She begged him to let the child live, and he did, but only at the center of a labyrinth as treacherous as her heart. The bull was slaughtered, and the queen wept.

‡

The bull is sacred and the bull is perverse.
The bull is unclean and the bull is purged with fire.
The bull's body is meat and bronze.
The bull is a god pretending to be a bull.

‡

Doomed love repeats itself like a pattern on cloth. Theseus, sent to slay the minotaur, felt his sword hand go soft. The beast's body was a blast furnace, wiping his mind clean. Its fur dark as venous blood, its chest a mosaic of lean muscle. Brazenly naked. Muzzle steaming like a bathhouse.

He thought of lying on his back, the bull's weight pouring over him like red sealing wax. He thought about setting fire to a thousand ships.

He found the center of the labyrinth but got lost in the chambers of his own heart. His infected heart with seams of pus. A bacterial fever confused as desire.

First he drained the wound. Then, tears simmering on his cheeks, he thrust the blade through the minotaur's velvet throat.

‡

I'm more maze than I am monster,
but sometimes I feel an old fury,
a horned head rising inside me.

‡

Ariadne held the ball of golden string as it unraveled into the labyrinth. Her heart went taut when the line did. As a princess, she had the luxury of monomaniacal love. If Theseus died, there would still be meat on her plate and sheets on her bed.

The minotaur's head emerged first, and then Theseus, embraced in its steaming blood. He would not kiss her or drop the dripping trophy.

What frightened her was not that he had changed, but that he had become himself. What frightened her was what she'd find if she followed her own labyrinth to its center.

‡

The man who built the labyrinth,
they say he was cunning. They say
his own invention outsmarted him.
They say the things we create
will someday destroy us.

‡

First there was a dancing pavilion. A limpid pool like a god's eye
in the center of the floor. Corinthian columns wreathed in purple
grapes. Everyone wore a crown of laurels. They were so good at
being rich.

At the king's command, the labyrinth was excavated beneath the
pavilion, and every year, seven boys and seven girls were sent to
sate the minotaur's hunger.

Don't worry. This is not your problem. Pour yourself a cup of wine
and dance on the bones of other people's children.

‡

I was born with the maze
but the monster came later.
I was so full of monster
I couldn't eat.

                    It made
a stockyard of my body.
The smell of slaughter
on my breath.
                    I thought
I had to kill myself to kill
the monster. But the monster
was only doing what the king
commanded it to do.
                    The king

must die.

          That was the night
          the bull grew horns.

My Imaginary Lover Is the Greatest Knight in the Land

When he came to our kingdom,
he was just a potato sack peasant
with a goatee of acne,
hair cut by shears and purse cut by urchins.
No one knew his name.

No one questions
his meteoric rise to stardom.
Men like him always make deals
with women like me, swearing
their perfect silence.

I give him knighthood
and he gives me his nights;
beneath a flowering thorn tree
he rides me like a palfrey.
Soon he will speak my name,

proclaim that my beauty
surpasses the queen's.
She will have him
on the chopping block for this.
Perhaps I shall save his life,

or perhaps I shall let him bleed.
It becomes a strange addiction,
claiming men's hearts,
then watching them
sally forth to die.

My Imaginary Lover Is a Wizard with the Appetites of Men

I make him teach me how
to conjure a great black warhorse,
how to disguise myself
as a beggar or a king.

I make him teach me augury.
He has seen a dragon
mapped in stars; he has
seen his own undoing.

He has cast
his last prophecy.
The next dragon he sees
will be me.

My Imaginary Lover Breeds Dragons (vi)

And I am the dragon.

Give me one good reason
why I can't be.

My turn to eat the moon.
My turn to bury great cities in ash.

I am the dragon.

You look so small to me now.
You have wasted so much of my time.

All this time spent seeking endlessness,
when all this time I was endlessness incarnate.

I am the dragon.

A ridge of ice down my spine.
Too bright, too colossal to gaze upon,
I am mostly ultraviolet.

You can't see me
but you feel me burning.

Author's Notes & Acknowledgments

"from My Imaginary Lover's Private Diary." A found poem composed of lines from *Lovebirds* by Matthew M. Vriends.

"Revelation Comes as a Lightning Bolt." Title taken from *78 Degrees of Wisdom* by Rachel Pollack.

"Dream Journal." Includes a quote from *The Element Encyclopedia of 20,000 Dreams* and lines from Maggie Nelson's *Bluets*.

"My Imaginary Lover Talks in His Sleep." A found poem composed of the Goblin King's lines in the movie *Labyrinth*.

"Tomorrowland." Borrows text from the Tomorrowland dedication plaque at Disneyland.

‡

"Where did this imaginary lover thing come from?" my mom asked after my MFA thesis defense. The question took me aback. Though I'd never articulated him before *Everything Is Real*, the imaginary lover has been my muse for as long as I can remember. I raise a glass of poisoned wine to you, my sexy gothic misanthrope plagued by inner demons. We finally did it. This is your book.

Endless gratitude to my advisors and colleagues at Oregon State University who helped bring this project to life. Jen, thank you for being the method to my madness. I couldn't have gotten this far without your editorial insights, killer prompts, and game-changing advice on organization.

Karen, thank you for fostering such a positive workshop environment and encouraging me to take risks, be playful, and trust my instincts.

75

Hannah and Alana, my tiny but mighty cohort, I learned so much about craft from your different voices and perspectives. Alana, "Pain Manifesto" is 100 percent an homage to "A Guide to Cages." Hannah, queen of erasures, your influence is all over the found poems in this collection.

Robin and Kayla, where would I be without you to talk me down from my poetic panics? Thank you both for the clarity, kindness, and comprehensiveness of your feedback. You are stellar readers and stellar-er friends.

Cohorts of 2015 and 2017, you brilliant human beings, thank you for always giving me a safe space to share my strange poetry experiments. What a treat to workshop with you.

And of course, massive thanks to the kind folks at Brain Mill for turning this long-lived fantasy into a reality.

About the Author

A graduate of Oregon State University's MFA program, Rita Feinstein is currently based in Washington, DC, where she teaches creative writing to kids and teens. Her stories and poems have appeared in *Permafrost*, *Grist*, and *Willow Springs*, among other publications, and have been nominated for Best of the Net and Best New Poets. She lives with her husband, who is a lawyer, and her dog, who is not.

CPSIA information can be obtained
at www.ICGtesting.com
Printed in the USA
LVHW081752011022
729734LV00004B/120